Iamatree

NOTE TO ADULTS

Who Am I? is a series of ten books illustrating a wide range of topics in natural science. The imaginative illustrations and simple text are designed to encourage children to consider different aspects of each topic. Parents or teachers can considerably increase children's understanding and enjoyment of the books by discussing each page with them. Many pages can also be used as starting points for imaginative story-telling not specifically related to the text.

At first I was very little.

I was a seed.

As the years went by
I grew into a plant.

My trunk was
harder than the
stem of a rose.

My leaves were
smaller than
cabbage leaves.

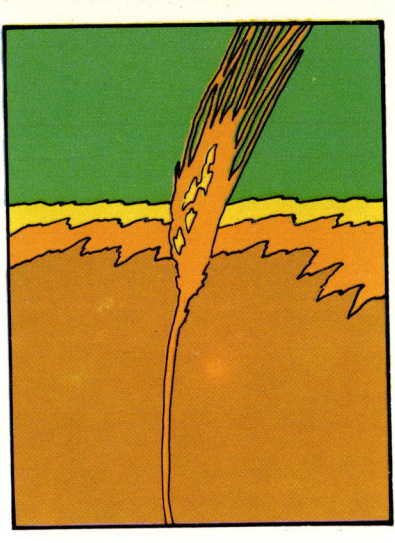

My roots were
stronger than
the roots of wheat

I was
thinner than
an oak

I was
slimmer than
a beech

and taller than
a Christmas tree.

My leaves were very important. They
helped me breathe. They helped to
clean the air. I had thousands of leaves . . .

Little leaves
in Spring

Very green leaves
in Summer

Brown leaves
in Autumn

No leaves
in Winter.

Time passed and I grew bigger and bigger.

Then one day I found
something beside me.

It was a female tree.

I wanted to be near her

but trees cannot walk.

I cannot move, but I can send messages

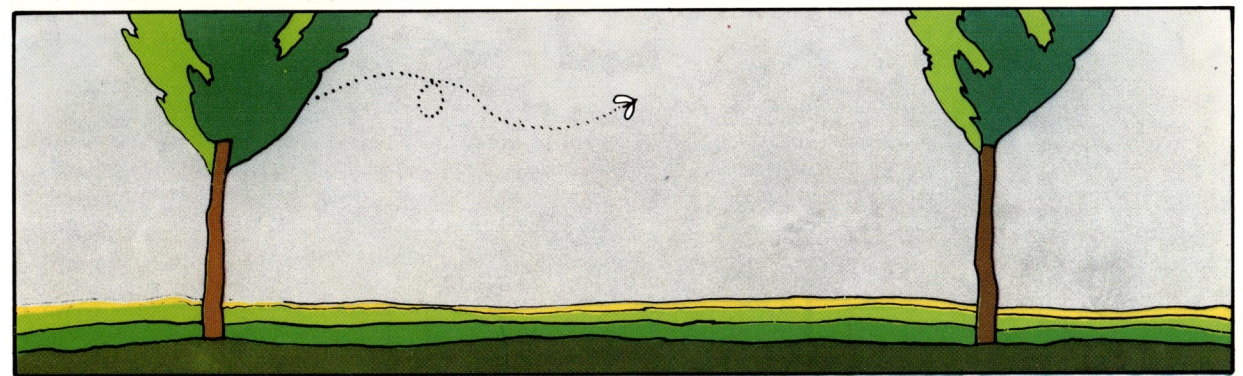

by insects

by birds

and by the wind.

With their help
we made many
other trees.

Together we made
a wood.

We were happy

with the owl

and the rabbits

and the fox

and the mushrooms

and the grass

and even with
Snow White's seven dwarfs.

People like woods.

They like the shade,
the animals,
the green grass
and the sunset.

But people also like cold drinks, reading
newspapers, smoking, and hunting birds and
animals.

One day a man came along and said :

He put up a notice.

e put a fence round the forest.

and had the trees chopped down so that he
could sell the wood from them to make
newspapers and other things.

I was the last to be chopped down.

With me were

  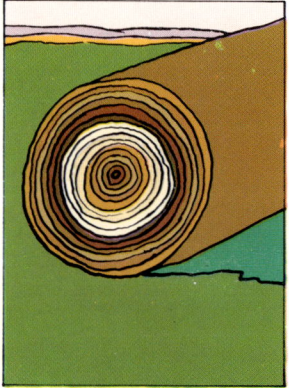 

one of my
children who was
180 years old

another child
who was
100 years old

a grandchild was
40 years old

another grandchild
was 25 years old

My friends, the birds, insects, squirrels, moles,
grass and mushrooms all came to say goodbye.

I was taken to a saw-mill.

The other trees were made into many useful things.

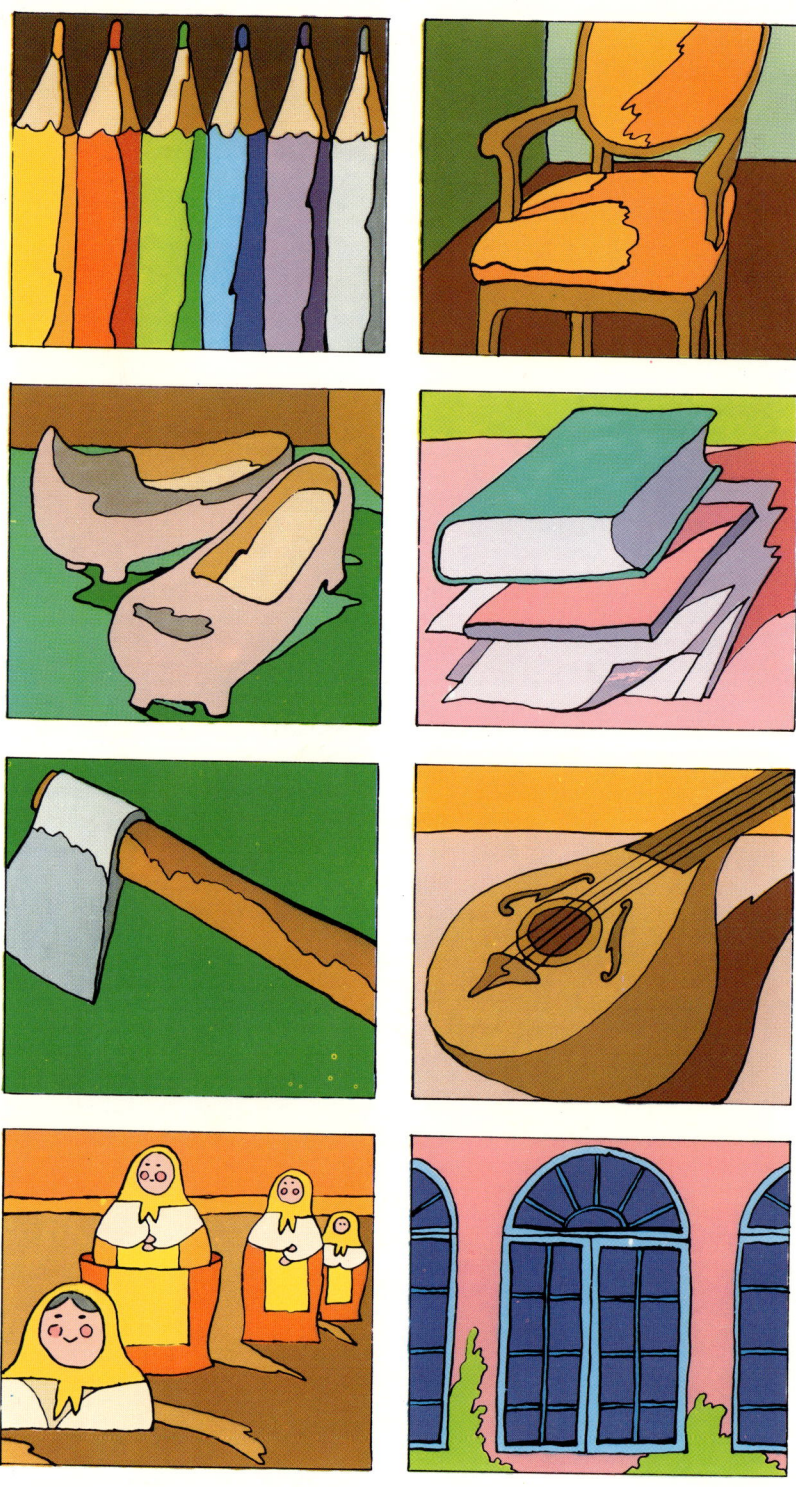

I stood alone in a field. I felt
bare and bored. Time passed.

After the snow of winter

spring came

with its rain and sunshine.

Trees feed by the roots when the earth is wet.

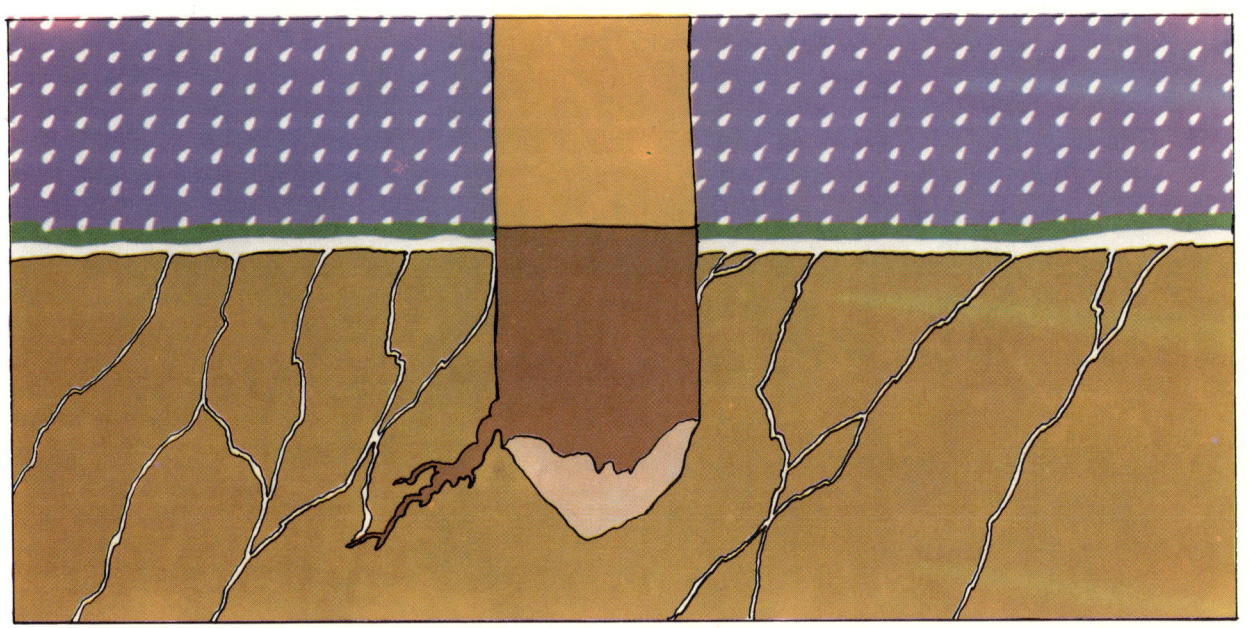

I think they must have left me a bit of root
because I began to feed again.

Then one day . . .

after many days,

many weeks

and many months

34

I felt like a tree again

and there was my wife beside me !

Now we are waiting for the birds, insects,
squirrels, moles, rabbits and mushrooms.
And perhaps the seven dwarfs will come too.